ECLECTIC STYLE

IN INTERIOR DESIGN

DESIGN: *Dutton & Sherman*

LAYOUT: *Sara Day Graphic Design*

First published in the United States of America by
Rockport Publishers, Inc.
33 Commercial Street
Gloucester, Massachusetts 01930
Telephone: (978) 282-9590
Fax: (978) 283-2742

Distributed to the book trade and art trade in the
United States by
North Light Books, an imprint of
F & W Publications
1507 Dana Avenue
Cincinnati, Ohio 45207
Telephone: (800) 289-0963

Other distribution by
Rockport Publishers, Inc.
Gloucester, Massachusetts 01930

ISBN 1-56496-413-2

10 9 8 7 6 5 4 3 2 1

Manufactured in China.

Dedicated to my mother and father, who first showed me that love was the essence of home, and to my husband David, with whom I live out that original blessing.

Many, many thanks to the editors and staff at Rockport Publishers, whose professional excellence is only enhanced by the fact that they are caring human beings. Acquisitions editor Rosalie Grattaroti's energy, vision, and ever-vibrant spirit were the lodestone and lodestar of *Eclectic Style*. The book's editor, Martha Wetherill, is remarkable for her quiet intelligence and sheer graciousness. The graphic design of Dutton & Sherman and Sara Day made the words and photographs come alive on the pages. Lucy Kohler and Jennie duMonde gave invaluable help in collecting material for the book.

In addition, I gratefully acknowledge John Aves of Vitae Publishing, who first conceived the idea of a book on eclectic design and provided assistance throughout the process. Janet Henderson of Eric Roth Studio also deserves recognition for her unflagging interest in the project and fine photo research.

Most of all, I extend my gratitude to the women and men whose work appears in *Eclectic Style*—the many superb photographers who painstakingly translate beauty to film, and the design professionals who care enough to create rooms that express the delightful quirks and unique passions of their clients.

—Carol Meredith

ECLECTIC STYLE

IN INTERIOR DESIGN

CAROL MEREDITH

ROCKPORT PUBLISHERS
GLOUCESTER, MASSACHUSETTS

CONTENTS

 REFACE

By Carol Meredith

Looking at the rooms featured in *Eclectic Style,* I am fascinated by the stories they tell. When design elements have been culled over the years from various styles and sources, an interior environment reads like the autobiography of the person who lives there. Every collected object, every angle, every corner is another page of the narrative.

In your own home, an eclectic approach to design offers the same potential for revealing who you are.

Where did you come from? What are the roots from which your life emerged? A colorful stack of patchwork quilts speaks eloquently of a great aunt who staunchly made the most of a little. An elegant Federal-era sofa and photographs of solemn forebears—men in stovepipe hats and women clad in lace and frills—remind another person of family roots in urban high society. In my own living room, my grandfather's handmade wooden toolbox, now polished and in a place of honor, calls to mind his humble, patient ways. Passed through generations, heirlooms such as these carry the spirit of those who have touched them along the way and help to tell the story of one's origins.

Beyond heirlooms, an eclectic mix can answer another, less remote question: In your own lifetime, where have you been? In the home of one woman, seashells and wave-worn

rocks serve as reminders of beach walks—brisk constitutionals with friends and solitary strolls to the distant cadence of ocean rhythms. In a gentleman's high-rise apartment, mementos of travels around the world leave a trail as telling as a passport. The objects that convey our personal domestic autobiographies are unique, from maps and books gathered in dusty back rooms of intriguing antiques shops, to modern paintings acquired after meeting up-and-coming artists at gallery openings, to Navajo pottery purchased during visits to the American West.

Beyond revealing where you came from and where you have been in your lifetime, eclectic design offers an opportunity to create a home that says much about who and what you love in life—the people, places, eras, aesthetic sensibility, and experiences that touch and connect with your passion, your heart, your deepest essence as a unique and precious individual.

Only then do the objects and elements brought together in a room transcend being mere decoration, rising to the realm of nurturing the people who live there on an emotional, psychological, and even spiritual level. Only then does "house" evolve into "home."

FOREWORD

Eclecticism: "I Did It My Way"
By Charles D. Gandy, FASID, IIDA

What is this thing we call eclecticism? Is it a style or a lifestyle? A look or an affection? A trend or a long-lasting tour de force? Whatever one decides, eclecticism seems here to stay. Now, with *Eclectic Style* one can begin to better understand this design phenomenon and not only learn to recognize it, but also to adapt or adopt it—to make it one's own.

Eclecticism can perhaps best be defined as a mixing of more than one style, combining objects from dissimilar sources and aesthetics into a whole. This simple definition explains the word, but the larger challenge is to define how eclectic spaces either succeed or fail.

Since humankind began decorating and adorning their living spaces, effective mixing has been the keystone in any successful interior. But until recent years, that mixing typically followed a set of rules that outlined, in more or less specific terms, the style or "look" that was being attempted. Only recently, since eclecticism has come to be a recognized approach to decorating and, in and of itself, a bona fide style, has this concept of "going by the rules" increasingly been eclipsed by an "anything goes" approach.

To trace when and how eclecticism emerged in the twentieth century, one need only look back a few decades to the era of the Beatles. In the 1960s, this revolutionary British rock group spawned a generation of freethinkers who rejected conformity in favor of independence. This new-found freedom, which we now take for granted, instigated a dramatic and evidently permanent change in almost every area of life.

Hairstyles, clothing, even our automobiles became an opportunity for personal expression (remember Volkswagen Bugs with daisy decals?). Rules were out, individualism was in. Soon this individual expressiveness found an outlet in our living spaces as well. No longer did we have to do things the way our parents had always done them. The untouched, unlived-in living room became an antiquated symbol of the past. Personal expression became the rule—the *only* rule, other than comfort.

As this new interior design movement came into being, numerous trade and shelter magazines began to document its existence, which had a snowball effect. The more the magazines showed this no-holds-barred approach to decorating, the more it was encouraged, accepted, and even expected. An educate public, filled with a sense of "I can and will do it *my* way," began to create spaces that reflected their lifestyle—a lifestyle with personality—and in doing so, eclecticism came into its own.

So how does one determine the success or failure of an eclectic space if, indeed, most of the old rules that directed design decisions have gone by the wayside? The answer lies in one word: quality. Both quality of the *abstract,* and quality of the *real.*

Abstract quality deals with those areas of design that are aesthetic in nature—line, rhythm, scale, balance, proportion, mass, pattern, texture, and color. These elements all interact to determine if an object in space is appropriate and contributes to a pleasing whole according to standards of the time. The proportions of the object in relationship to others, its relative placement, color, texture, line, and form, all combine to create the overall result.

But it takes more than abstract quality alone for an interior design to succeed. Quality of the real is also essential. Is the level of each object appropriate and consistent with all the others? This does not mean that every decorative item in an eclectic space need be an expensive one. Rather, it means that each item needs, in some important sense, to be on a par with the others. And although several elements in a given space may come from totally different perspectives, they can and should be able to hold their own when standing alone. For example, an impressive contemporary painting becomes even stronger when properly placed over an exquisite eighteenth-century settee. In this case, both pieces represent the best of their time, and thus they work together as well as alone.

Enough said, because eclecticism isn't about rules. Instead, it is a remarkable opportunity for people to express their personality in the designed environment. The more personality expressed, the better the space.

Eclecticism indeed is here to stay. Bravo! Through this exciting approach to design, the personal aspect of every individual is celebrated and preserved. At last, we can express and create our own style—and have fun doing it.

LD WITH NEW

With references to periods and styles of the past, traditional houses are design's equivalent of comfort food—familiar and substantial, known to nourish and sustain over time. Typically, the overall ambiance of these interiors seems closed-in and nest-like rather than open and airy. Furniture and furnishings reference historical styles, and with the past comes a comforting sense of nostalgia.

Certainly one of the appeals of traditional design is the hope of longevity. No one wants to purchase a piece of furniture today that will seem outdated tomorrow. Antiques and reproductions offer time-tested approaches to materials and finishes, line and form, scale and proportion.

Blend eclectic style with traditionalism, and the hope of longevity becomes a veritable promise. By incorporating items from various eras and locales rather than adhering to one strict period style, an interior effectively avoids all possibilities of becoming dated. Particularly when the various eras include our own—the very recent past and present day.

But timelessness is just one of the appeals of mixing an occasional new piece with old-style furniture. Another is the way new furniture, objects, and artwork add sparkle and interest to traditional rooms. In a context of gleaming hardwood furniture, the polished chromium-plated, curved steel tubes of a twentieth-century chair designed by the great Marcel Breuer seem particularly vibrant. Or consider the abstract painting that offers welcome respite to an otherwise literal and predictable room.

With a palette of gold, orange, and green, color is the constant in this room that pairs traditional furniture with contemporary art.

INTERIOR DESIGN
Jean Valente

Photo: Charles Lewis

Perhaps the most important reason of all to take an eclectic approach to primarily traditional rooms is this: Incorporating the well-chosen new item amid classic and period pieces shifts the emphasis away from style to quality. And you simply can't go wrong surrounding yourself with belongings that represent the best of their time. That, in and of itself, says much about who you are and how you strive to live your life.

Subtle taupe and ivory weave
throughout this peaceful oasis
that blends fine antiques with
well-chosen pieces of contemporary furniture and art. Note
how the large Biedermeier secretary and over-scaled contemporary painting balance one
another through their careful
placement.

INTERIOR DESIGN

Gandy/Peace

Photos: Chris A. Little

In the midst of ornate furniture and opulent fabrics, a single modern piece, such as a small table, provides a refreshing point of contrast.

INTERIOR DESIGN
Carol Wolk Interiors

Photo: James W. Hedrich, Hedrich Blessing

The dreamlike quality of the artwork adds a contemporary layer to the bedroom's romantic decor.

INTERIOR DESIGN
Stacey Lapuk

Photos: John Sutton Photography

A handsome study features a
contemporary desk whose rich
woods and inlay styling are con-
sonant with the room's traditional look, but whose sleek
lines set it pleasingly apart.

INTERIOR DESIGN

Coursey Design Consultants

Photo: Rob Karosis

The ideal proportion and scale
of the furnishings and the walls
of books in this eclectic room
add to the peaceful, well-
ordered effect.

INTERIOR DESIGN

Thomas Pheasant

Photo: Gordon Beall

(below) The easy elegance of this room is enhanced by understated window treatments that allow for clear views and sunlight.

INTERIOR DESIGN

Stacey Lapuk

Photo: John Sutton

(right) From old tapestries and traditional furnishings to modern artwork and a gleaming coffee table, this room exemplifies the layered look typical of spaces created as a result of the owners' evolving tastes.

INTERIOR DESIGN

Designs by Billy W. Francis and Ed Russell

Photo: Peter Vitali

Although French and Chinese antiques domi-
nate, a contemporary painting fits in beautifully
with the room's golden hues.

INTERIOR DESIGN

Rodger Dobbel Interiors

Photo: David Livingston

(above) While this interior is primarily traditional, the occasional modern artwork or furnishing defies predictability.

INTERIOR DESIGN
Thomas C. Achille and Associates

Photo: Mary Nichols

(right) An alcove adjacent to the grand entry of a European-style residence breaks from the past with two whimsical triangular tables.

INTERIOR DESIGN
Anna Meyers Interiors

At first glance, the dark wood paneling gives the
impression of a steeped-in-tradition gentleman's
club. The artwork, dramatically lit ceiling, and
much of the furniture, however, dispel any hint
of stuffiness.

INTERIOR DESIGN

Celeste Cooper

Photo: Richard Mandelkorn

(below) Furniture and objects from various eras happily coexist in this striking space, as do a variety of intriguing textures—the polish of faux marble moldings and varnished wooden beams, and the subtle weave of the damask wall covering and sofa pillows.

INTERIOR DESIGN
McWhorter Associates

Photo: Joey Terrill

(right) A new glass-topped iron table is home to diverse objects featuring natural colors.

INTERIOR DESIGN
Paul Magnuson

Photo: Eric Roth

The objects in this Victorian-era home span
the centuries. The contemporary sculpture
from New Mexico and the highly saturated
colors of the walls, tablecloth, and rug add to
the lively mix.

INTERIOR DESIGN

Alfred J. Walker Fine Art

Photo: Eric Roth

(below) Gold and silver bring richness to this bedroom, which blends classic furniture with the small, avant-garde table next to the chaise.

INTERIOR DESIGN

Celeste Cooper

Photo: Richard Mandelkorn

(right) The design approach is traditional, with new upholstered pieces that provide comfortable seating and support the palette of earth tones.

INTERIOR DESIGN

Designs by Billy W. Francis and Ed Russell

Photo: H. Durston Saylor

A perfect example of an eclectic room that
succeeds because each element, whether traditional or contemporary, is of high quality.

INTERIOR DESIGN
Stedila Design

Photo: Alec Hemer

(below) Some of the best accent pieces are both similar and dissimilar to the surrounding furniture. Here, the simple lines of the small, red, three-legged side table are in keeping with the other furniture's lines, yet the table's modern attitude and color are eye-catching.

INTERIOR DESIGN

Bloomingdale's

Photo: Richard Mandelkorn

(right) Introducing a bold, modern fabric quickens the pulse of any room.

INTERIOR DESIGN

Bierly-Drake Associates

Photo: Sam Gray

Amid a very eclectic interior that blends everything from Victorian to cottage-style furniture, a simple, modern coffee table fits right in.

INTERIOR DESIGN
Duquette and Company

Photo: Rob Karosis

An abstract painting and modern sculpture add spice to this pleasing, low-key space.

INTERIOR DESIGN
John Robert Wiltgen

Photo: Steve Hall, Hedrich Blessing

(*left*) In a bedroom with lots of personal style, the dressing table's mirror is flanked by hinged panels of old architectural prints. The dressing chair incorporates a playful modern take on a classic Roman chair base.

INTERIOR DESIGN

Deborah M. Roub

Photo: Rob Karosis

(*below*) Clean, white accents and dining chairs similar to outdoor furniture give this sunny space the casual breeziness of a garden room.

INTERIOR DESIGN

Paul Magnuson

Photo: Eric Roth

(below) While the architecture speaks of yesterday, the leather sofas designed by Magistretti make a resounding statement about the present.

Photo courtesy of Cassina USA

(right) This interior is grounded firmly in the past, except for a single marble-topped table whose modern styling adds character and sparkle to the space.

INTERIOR DESIGN

Arlis Ede Interiors

Photo: John Rogers

Each piece of artwork lends its own unique atmosphere to the different areas of this primarily traditional home.

INTERIOR DESIGN

Samuel Botero Associates

Photo: Phillip H. Ennis

(right, below, and opposite) This superb living room hosts an exuberant meeting of classical, rococo, and contemporary styles. Note how the fabrics and upholstery alternate between the past and present.

INTERIOR DESIGN

Barry Dixon

Photos: Gordon Beall

(below) The duo of elegantly understated contemporary chairs and an unadorned wooden music stand balance the more ornate elements of this Victorian-era home's architecture and patterned carpets and fabrics.

INTERIOR DESIGN

Lloy Hack Associates

Photo: Andrew D. Lautman

(right) Formal pieces used in casual ways can be very effective and even witty. Along the wall at the left, a priest's vestment cabinet from the Middle Ages now serves as a liquor cabinet.

INTERIOR DESIGN

Barry Dixon

Photo: Gordon Beall

Each of the pieces in this living room has an appeal of its
own—the leather gilded chair; a time-worn but still-prim
upholstered stool; and the linear, low-backed modern
sofa covered with a paisley throw. As an ensemble, they
convey the owner's confident sense of eclectic style.

Photo: Jean Allsopp

With its unusual curved shape, an antique tall
clock seems like a piece of sculpture in this
otherwise contemporary room.

INTERIOR DESIGN

Françoise Theise for Adesso Furniture

Photo: Eric Roth

NEW WITH OLD

People who seek out that which is new, whether in work or play, mind or spirit—as well as in interior design—possess a certain courage. From the French word *coeur,* meaning heart, courage involves unique vitality, an inner vibrancy that energizes true modernists' willingness to embrace the present and future.

In the world of interior design, the new consists not only of the latest in furniture and furnishings, but also much of the design of the twentieth century. What's new, when seen in the context of interior design and architecture over the ages, is a refreshing departure from historical references, excessive clutter, and ornamentation applied solely for its own sake. Rather than celebrating abundance and fullness on every surface and in every corner, a contemporary aesthetic favors visual restraint achieved by a selective paring down.

At its core, contemporary design is basic and elemental. Light and shadow are verbs rather than nouns—animated design elements emerging and receding in an ongoing dance. Textures are subtle but nonetheless make their presence known. Color typically is used judiciously, perhaps in monochromatic schemes of neutrals or in solid expanses of saturated hues. Clear, straightforward line and form are recognized for their inherent, simple beauty.

(right) The clean-lined sculpture niche, red boxed-beam ceiling, and unembellished columns are all decidedly contemporary, but antique Hitchcock dining chairs still seem right at home. In the hallway, Thos. Moser Cabinetmakers' modern take on a Windsor chair brings new and old together in hand-rubbed cherry wood.

INTERIOR ARCHITECTURE

Theodore and Theodore Architects

Photo: Eric Roth

In an elegant entry hall of a
contemporary residence, each
furnishing item is surrounded
by ample space. As a result,
antiques as well as whimsical
new art furniture take on the
commanding quality of objects
in a gallery.

INTERIOR ARCHITECTURE

Olson Lewis & Dioli Architects

Photo: Eric Roth

As wonderful as a purely modern setting can be, some of the most intriguing rooms are contemporary spaces that incorporate pieces of the past. In these primarily new rooms, a reference to yesterday acts as an accent or anchor, depending on comparative visual weight. With its solemn grayness and elaborately carved frame, an heirloom family portrait becomes a focal point. A single piece of antique furniture, with its figured woods and sinuous shape, takes on the aura of a graceful sculpture.

By setting up an unexpected contrast between new and old elements, interior design can accentuate the differences between then and now. As a result, the people who live with the room are subtly encouraged to celebrate both what was and what is.

(left) Choice antiques become the focal point in a sparsely furnished, monochromatic contemporary space.

INTERIOR DESIGN
Veronique Louvet

Photo: Eric Roth

(below) The cool restraint of modern architecture provides a quiet envelope for antiques from various periods. Proportion and scale are important issues in soaring rooms, which call for large-scale artwork and furniture.

INTERIOR ARCHITECTURE
Olson Lewis & Dioli Architects

Photo: Eric Roth

(below) Old-time cabinetwork details, chrome pulls, and glass-paneled cabinet fronts create a comfortable ambiance in this kitchen. In keeping with an overall modern sensibility, a structural steel beam was incorporated into the design like a found object.

INTERIOR ARCHITECTURE
Theodore and Theodore Architects

Photo: Eric Roth

(right) This kitchen blends the sleek appeal of modern cabinetry and granite with feathery plants and a quaint display of old teapots and collectibles. The window's glass shelving obscures a less-than-appealing exterior view without obstructing natural light.

INTERIOR ARCHITECTURE
Jonathan Fishman

KITCHEN DESIGN
Nancy Tavel Balbus

Photo: Andrew D. Lautman

A sharp contrast between light and dark draws attention
to an asymmetrical antique couch in this high-rise
apartment.

INTERIOR DESIGN
Arlis Ede Interiors

Photo: John Rogers

Twentieth-century elegance
welcomes the classic styling of
the antique armchairs.

INTERIOR DESIGN

Celeste Cooper

Photo: Richard Mandelkorn

Contemporary in its simplicity.
this room flirts with traditional
details in the fireplace surround
and classical caned bench.

INTERIOR DESIGN
Gandy/Peace

Photo: Chris A. Little

(below) Antiques accent a space that exudes a cutting-edge attitude.

INTERIOR DESIGN
Freya Serabian

Photo: Steve Vierra

(right) Combining a modern curved desk and classical appointments creates an attractive home office that defies categorization.

INTERIOR DESIGN
Judith Lynne

Photo: Ethan Kaminsky

A richly patterned antique Savonnerie carpet is
enhanced by the streamlined forms and compatible
tones of the dining-room furniture.

INTERIOR DESIGN
Gayle Shaw Camden

Photo: Balthazar Korab

This comfortable golden sitting room establishes a
personal style through a liberated mix of objects
and pattern.

INTERIOR DESIGN

Camille Belmonte and Mary Beth Galvin, Wellesley Design Center

Photo: Steve Vierra

(left) The owners' idiosyncratic approach to pattern and color is grounded by the warm wood tones of an occasional antique.

INTERIOR DESIGN
C & J Katz Studio

Photo: Eric Roth

(below) An antique gilt armchair punctuates the modern furnishings of this delightfully unique study. Notice how natural light draws the eye to the sculptures flanking the space.

INTERIOR DESIGN
Judy McMurray

Photo: Steve Vierra

In a house with many contemporary furnishings, the
dining room furniture looks back rather than forward.
Though traditional in effect, the dining room table and
chairs stay connected to the surroundings through classical details that echo the interior architectural columns.

INTERIOR DESIGN

Lloy Hack Associates

Photo: Warren Jagger Photography

A massive antique pool table with inlaid and carved
detailing provides visual ballast in an open-concept
house with soaring volumes of space.

INTERIOR DESIGN

Rita St. Clair

Photo: Deborah Mazzoleni

In a room that reverberates with color and youthful energy, an antique sideboard's lean, well-defined look harmonizes with clean-lined contemporary furniture. The sideboard's lack of applied molding is typical of the Federal era.

INTERIOR DESIGN
Marcia Connors and Roxy Gray, Growing Spaces

Photos: Steve Vierra

Color is an effective way to link eclectic items together.
Here, black is the common denominator of the Empire
chandelier, traditional chairs, and modern table.

INTERIOR DESIGN
Thomas C. Achille and Associates

Photo: Mary Nichols

Modern art, new furniture, and the unexpected red
color of the mantel add personal flair to a house with
traditional architecture.

INTERIOR DESIGN

Ida Goldstein

Photo: Steve Vierra

(left) This eclectic living room works in large part because of its unifying color scheme of red, brown, gold, and soft yellow.

INTERIOR DESIGN
Samuel Botero Associates

Photo: Phillip H. Ennis

(below) The fine woods of the new paneling, traditional table, and eighteenth-century-style chairs all cast a vibrant glow in this dining room.

INTERIOR DESIGN
Howard Snoweiss Design Group

Photo: Steven Brooke

(above and opposite) Through the addition of antique textiles and accessories, the owner's love of the old is satisfied within the context of a contemporary look.

INTERIOR DESIGN

Solis Betancourt

Photos: Andrew D. Lautman

(right) Huge antique frames leaning against the wall add an intriguing touch to a contemporary bedroom.

Photo courtesy of Charles P. Rogers Brass and Iron Beds

(below) Touches of antiquity enhance this bedroom whose central feature is a modern version of a canopy bed.

Photo courtesy of Charles P. Rogers Brass and Iron Beds

Amid a sea of pristine white, the owner's ebony antique
desk and collection of art catch the eye and become the
focus of the room.

INTERIOR DESIGN
Al Evans Interiors

Photo: Dan Forer

(below) A large, antique, Chinese camphorwood cabinet matches the room's scale while adding a layer from another time and place.

INTERIOR DESIGN
McWhorter Associates

Photo: Michael Garland

(right) A mirror with a white ornate frame sits amidst a modern bedroom's earthy colors with such casual aplomb that it seems like a found object.

INTERIOR DESIGN
Cann & Company

Photo: Eric Roth

An antique birdcage, capital table bases, and bare stone
wall add accents from bygone eras to an otherwise
contemporary bedroom.

Guest room at Auberge St. Antoine

Photo: Rob Karosis

Contemporary architecture serves as a clean, uncluttered backdrop for an eclectic blend of pieces tied
together by their neutral colors. A glass-block wall *(opposite)* is juxtaposed with traditional furniture, establishing a
sophisticated yet down-to-earth style.

INTERIOR DESIGN

Annelle Primos

Photos: Tom Joynt

(below) The Oriental screen and black-and-white striped Empire-style chairs from Spain are in perfect accord with the neutral color scheme, which is a constant in this high-rise condominium.

INTERIOR DESIGN
Lloy Hack Associates

Photo: Steve Rosenthal

(right) A prime antique, such as the beautiful wooden bed, and complementary patterns add unmistakable quality to this contemporary room.

INTERIOR DESIGN
Stingray Hornsby

Photo: Dennis Krukowski

The cabinetry is 1990s-vintage and the kitchen table
and chairs are from the 1950s. But an old wooden post
exposed when the space was gutted serves as a
reminder of the distant past.

Photo: Rob Karosis

The metal and wood blend of the tables, contemporary lines of the furniture, and narrow shelf along the wall displaying old treasures, such as a scale and wooden boxes, work well together.

INTERIOR DESIGN
Mark Zeff

Photo: Mario Ruiz

An exciting look emerges when furnishings from the past meet the innovative architecture of the present. The hard-edged zigzag of the stairs is softened by a warm, colorful grouping of simply-styled furnishings.

INTERIOR DESIGN
Cann & Company

Photos: Eric Roth

With its exuberant fluidity, tropical botanical fabric maintains a crispness that works well with the time-honored styling of the chairs and lamps. The fabric design is by Josef Frank, one of the founders of Swedish Modernism.

Photo courtesy of Brunschwig & Fils

The simplicity of a modern envelope showcases the
room's more ornate features such as traditional chairs
and a desk with rococo styling.

INTERIOR DESIGN

CBT/Childs Bertman Tseckares

Photo: Richard Mandelkorn

COLLECTOR'S MIX

(opposite) Collections tell a story about the people who live with them. In this historic New England home, heirlooms passed through generations speak of a venerable past, from family portraits to a wooden water bucket, now hanging from the ceiling, used to douse fires by an eighteenth-century relative. Pedigree makes way for playfulness on the stairway, where the owner's collection of antique miniature chests whimsically climbs the steps.

Photo: Eric Roth

(right) A collection of bold, contemporary art and a flash of neon on the ceiling transform a traditional room with high-energy results.

Photo: Eric Roth

As nineteenth-century English architecture critic John Ruskin noted, "Much of the character of every man may be read in his house." More specifically, your character can be read in the decorative objects you collect and gather together.

While interiors with a collected look offer extensive opportunities for personal expression, they also require serious consideration of the basics of visual presentation. Interior design elements such as placement, lighting, and color are important in any eclectic room, but particularly so in a space focusing on collections.

Collectors' interiors fall into two broad categories. Many have an overall aesthetic of abundance, an approach that can be summed up as "planned clutter" with numerous groupings on nearly every space and surface. In contrast, some collectors prefer interiors with a gallery-like quality, rooms that provide a simple, clean, and highly edited background that allows one or more collections to be undisputedly in the forefront.

No matter which approach you take, choices about organizing objects are key. When items are small, for instance, they should be displayed together in a group or they will all but disappear. Within a group, organize objects by size, height, shape, color, type, or some other salient quality.

A husband's and wife's lives come together in this room, where antiques passed down through his family blend with her collections of Balinese puppets and metalwork from her native Near East. Corbusier coffee tables add yet another dimension to the look.

INTERIOR DESIGN
Lloy Hack Associates

Photo: Eric Roth

When designing a room of collections, use accent lighting, also called decorative lighting, to draw attention to special objects. This can be in the form of lights installed within shelf units, ceiling illumination systems that throw light on wall displays, or small lamps that direct light down to a grouping on a tabletop. Placing objects in a way that makes use of natural light also is a fine way to draw attention to a collection during daytime hours.

When a gallery-like approach is taken, color should be used sparingly in the room. Monochromatic backgrounds in neutrals such as ivory or soft taupe are always effective. Limit the number of saturated colors to keep the focus on the collection, not the colors.

After all, the point is that objects painstakingly gathered over the years were purchased because they evoked something meaningful and vital in the collector. At best, the items are nothing less than beloved. Once acquired, they deserve to be displayed to best advantage, treated with honor and respect.

(left) An owner's interest in plants becomes a theme when translated into paintings and a living collection of topiaries and other potted greenery.

INTERIOR DESIGN
Charles Spada

Photo: Eric Roth; styling by Gwen Simpkins

(below) Antique photographs work beautifully in this sleek environment. Frames and mats are in keeping with the neutral palette, and careful placement supports the family room's overall impression of precision. Best of all, the collection speaks of the owner's love of sailing.

INTERIOR DESIGN
Gandy/Peace

Photo: Chris A. Little

(below) The owner's affinity for animals is evident in this parlor corner, which features a collection of dog figurines and a grouping of pastoral paintings with a bovine bent. Massing small collectibles together creates a distinct point of interest in an interior.

INTERIOR DESIGN

Elizabeth Speert

Photo: Eric Roth

(right) Stacked displays of artwork and decorative objects create a vertical rhythm in this space.

INTERIOR DESIGN

Charles Baker

Photo: Eric Roth

Using a treasured collection as the basis for a color
scheme ensures a unified look. Here, decorative tiles
inspired a palette of earth tones.

INTERIOR DESIGN

Andrew Reczkowski for Bloomingdale's

Photo: Eric Roth

(below) Black leather upholstery, pale taupe walls, and a design characterized by cool restraint allow modern art and multicultural artifacts to take center stage.

INTERIOR DESIGN
Sally Sirkin Lewis

Photo: Jaime Ardiles-Arce

(right) With its two-toned palette and chairs in a classical motif, this room's design derives from a fascinating collection of Greek vases and pitchers. Vertical display stands add visual emphasis to the collection, which might otherwise be dwarfed by the arched doors and high ceiling.

INTERIOR DESIGN
Solis Betancourt

Photo: Walter Smalling Jr., courtesy of House Beautiful

Gilt-framed engravings from the eighteenth and nine-
teenth centuries lighten a wood-paneled room. Close
groupings such as this one draw attention to a treasured
collection.

INTERIOR DESIGN
Annelle Primos & Associates

Photo: Tom Joynt

(right) Some of the most striking collections come straight from nature. Echoing the smooth texture of a marble-top table, sea stones hold memories of walks along the beach.

INTERIOR DESIGN

Charles Spada

Photo: Eric Roth; styling by Gwen Simpkins

(below) The entryway of this East Coast townhouse is a study in vertical and horizontal lines, with crisp geometry in the stairs, balusters, mullions, and paneled doors and walls. Sculpted and carved heads in relief punctuate the rhythm of the woodwork and seem to oversee the inhabitants' comings and goings.

INTERIOR DESIGN

C & J Katz Studio

Photo: Eric Roth

In a child's bedroom, a high shelf of old-time toys and advertising signs provides a neat, out-of-the-way display area. By dividing the space with a horizontal line, the shelf also diminishes the room's sense of scale.

INTERIOR DESIGN

Dawn Southworth and Dana Salvo

Photo: Eric Roth

(above) An ivory background and track lighting combine to create an elegant gallery-like space for framed art and sculpture.

Photo: Rob Karosis

(right) Miniature wooden chairs juxtaposed with a life-size chair give this corner a whimsical touch.

INTERIOR DESIGN
Bierly-Drake Associates

Photo: Sam Gray

For many people, the collected look translates into abundance. Leaning artwork against walls and stacking books on tables and chairs creates a casual, unaffected ambiance.

Photo: Eric Roth

(below) Baskets hanging from the ceiling of this country-style kitchen are both decorative and functional.

INTERIOR DESIGN
Decorative Interiors

Photo: Steve Vierra

(right) Built-in display alcoves with internal lighting work well for collectors who prefer uncluttered surroundings.

INTERIOR DESIGN
Ida Goldstein

Photo: Steve Vierra

With striking colors and patterns, American quilts stand
out against the white sofa. In a room of rough-hewn
wooden beams, old-time patchwork enhances the rustic
quality of the space.

INTERIOR DESIGN

Stan Topol & Associates

Photo: Kevin C. Rose

Considerations about how to display a collection are
every bit as important as decisions about individual acquisitions. A shelving system with mirrored backing and side
lights intensifies the impact of any collection.

INTERIOR DESIGN
Geoffrey N. Bradfield

Photo: H. Durston Saylor

The owners' appreciation of the ocean-front view goes hand-in-hand with a penchant for the luminous blues and greens of their glass collection. Colors become even more prominent when they are echoed by accent cushions and the objects are placed on glass shelves with a mirrored back.

INTERIOR DESIGN

Al Evans Interiors

Photo: Dan Forer

Identically matted and framed eighteenth-century Dutch
engravings cover the entire stairway wall, making a powerful impact in this grand entry. The collector obviously
has a keen appreciation of this art form.

INTERIOR DESIGN
Rodgers Menzies

Photo: Ira Montgomery

Collections of heirloom family photographs add a welcome sense of personal history to any home. On this bedroom wall, the images are matted against various floral backgrounds in identical gold frames to create a unique display. The rest of the room is a charming blend of antiques gathered over the years.

INTERIOR DESIGN

Kenneth Hockin Interior Decoration

Photos: William Stites

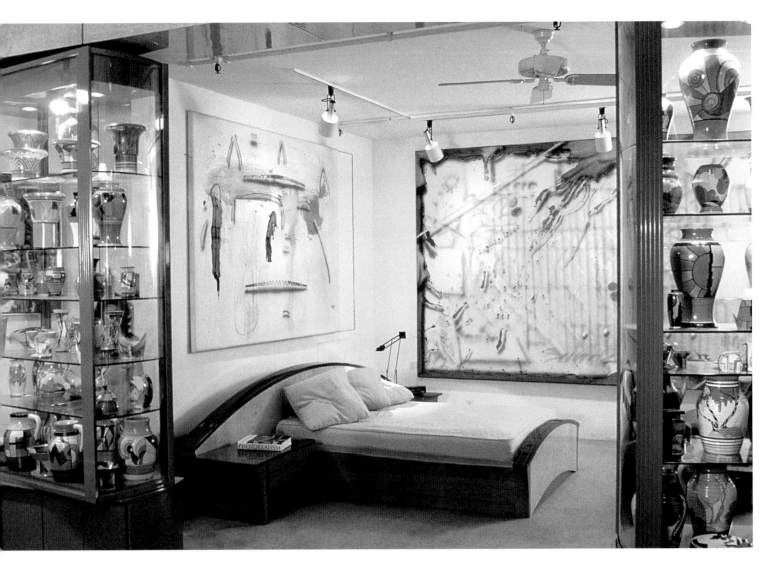

(above and left) Track lighting and soft background colors keep the emphasis on collections of art and pottery. Display cases with glass on four sides allow the pottery to be seen from adjacent spaces without interfering with the sense of openness.

Room by Dakota Jackson

(opposite) When a collection becomes the theme for an entire room, the impact intensifies. Colorful ceramics in a corner cupboard and on the table are accompanied by the fanciful wallpaper, fabrics, and chandelier.

INTERIOR DESIGN
Karen Sugarman Interiors

Photo: Eric Roth

(below and opposite) This study makes a personal statement with two collections: English statehouse china above the fireplace, and maritime paintings and models. Strong red walls help ground the room and unify its many facets.

Photos: Eric Roth

(right) A corner cabinet is a charming way to integrate china and glassware handed down through the generations. The yellow walls and creamy chair are in pleasant contrast with the darker, rich look of the other items in the room.

INTERIOR DESIGN
Kenneth Hockin Interior Decoration

Photo: Peter Margonelli

Incorporating one or two strong design elements creates focus in rooms teeming with objects and collectibles. In this parlor, the most powerful elements are red walls and one large piece of art.

INTERIOR DESIGN
Claude Guidi

Photo: Steve Vierra

This tasteful room tells a tale of a sophisticated owner
who loves to collect artwork and items from the Orient.

INTERIOR DESIGN

Sandra Nunnerley

Photos: Jaime Ardiles-Arce

(below) Symmetry can bring a sense of calm to an environment. The objects displayed on either side of the settee virtually mirror one another.

INTERIOR DESIGN
Lowrance Interiors

Photo: Charles White

(right) Rich gold unifies the accessories in this traditional living room, while the flowers and the fringed pillows maintain a sense of softness.

INTERIOR DESIGN
Karen Sugarman Interiors

Photo: Sam Gray

A child's charming bedroom features a fun collection of
toys and stuffed animals, an attitude that carries through
to the flora and fauna painted on the furniture.

INTERIOR DESIGN

Coursey Design Consultants

Photo: Rob Karosis

Honoring an outstanding collection of modern art, the interior designer of this Florida residence minimized clutter and carefully controlled the intensity of the neutral color palette. Artwork punctuates the space at regular intervals, resulting in a sense of balance.

INTERIOR DESIGN

Geoffrey N. Bradfield

Photo: H. Durston Saylor

A lively collection of contemporary artwork is supported
by pillows in the cubist style. The bold colors and odd
shapes of the pieces in the room work well together.

INTERIOR DESIGN

John Robert Wiltgen

Photo: Jon Miller, Hedrich Blessing

Serving as established focal points, fireplace mantels are prime spots for displaying collections. Blue-and-white porcelain transforms this simple wooden mantel.

Photo: Steve Vierra

(left) The colors of the porcelain collection carry through into the room's fabrics, while the orange pillows and soft peach walls add warmth to the scene.

INTERIOR DESIGN
Mario Buatta

(below) A room of serious heirlooms is brightened by butter-yellow walls and accented by the blues of the tiles and porcelain ware.

INTERIOR DESIGN
Josef Pricci

Photo: Bill Rothschild

This stairway, with its high expanse of
wall space and natural light, invites the-
matic displays of prints and artwork.

INTERIOR DESIGN
Susan Zises Green

Photo: Eric Roth

In the living room of this residence, a collection of framed images is given emphasis mounted on a blue-tinted glass mirror. Vintage bowling balls from the 1940s are treated like moveable pieces of art. In the dining room *(right)*, a collection of Robert Mapplethorpe photographs are juxtaposed with a pop-art cabinet with custom-designed buffet wings. The colors of the cabinet and buffet are picked up in the horizontal stripes of the crown molding, which is painted to resemble the coat of a dalmatian.

INTERIOR DESIGN
Al Evans Interiors

Photos: Dan Forer

(below) In this sitting area, richly textured and patterned textiles are a collection in and of themselves. Even the wallpaper border, which depicts draped fabric and tassels, plays out the theme.

INTERIOR DESIGN
Alfred J. Walker Fine Art

Photo: Eric Roth

(right) Narrow shelving wrapped around a room's perimeter accommodates an art aficionado's collection and encourages frequent rearranging as inspiration strikes.

INTERIOR DESIGN
Vicente Wolf Associates

Photo: Vicente Wolf

In this unusual presentation of a collection, reproductions
of old prints were applied directly to the walls of a hall
alcove.

INTERIOR DESIGN

Henry Johnstone & Co.

Photo: Alexander Vertikoff

These collectibles and decorative elements are perfectly balanced around the French screen and Italian console.

INTERIOR DESIGN
Rodgers Menzies

Photo: Ira Montgomery

(left) A new octagonal mirror reflects a wonderful antique clock, while a contemporary painting adds yet another dimension to the owner's diverse aesthetic sensibility.

INTERIOR DESIGN
Samuel Botero Associates

Photo: Phillip H. Ennis

(below) With niches and proper lighting, hallways can be transformed into gallery-like spaces to showcase diverse collections of art and artifacts.

INTERIOR DESIGN
Celeste Cooper

Photo: Richard Mandelkorn

Surely the owners of this room
are every bit as multifaceted and
colorful as the objects they have
in their living space.

INTERIOR DESIGN
Constance Driscoll Design Consultants

Photos: Eric Roth

Rescued from a corner of an attic, old-fashioned suit-
cases make a charming coffee table that brings even
more personality to this eclectic setting.

INTERIOR DESIGN

Paul Magnuson

Photo: Eric Roth

CROSS-CULTURAL STYLE

(opposite) An exquisite twelve-panel Coromandel screen completely changes the ambiance of this room with contemporary and traditional furnishings.

INTERIOR DESIGN
Weixler, Peterson & Luzi

Photo: Dan Forer

(right) The sense of dining al fresco, perhaps on an exotic seacoast or tropical island, is evoked by the vibrant painting, sponged terra-cotta walls, and valances designed to look like awnings.

INTERIOR DESIGN
Samantha Cole

Photo: Christopher Irion

In an age when modern transportation and technology continue to bring once distant ends of the globe closer together, blending objects and collections from various cultures is more popular than ever. When the items are purchased while visiting a foreign country, they act as mementos in three dimensions. Incorporating these treasures into our homes evokes memories of the places we have been and how they have changed us.

Today, of course, sensitive travelers strive to enter other lands and regions with the utmost respect for the native people and their culture. But many of the men who first brought objects home from foreign areas had quite the opposite approach. Ever since warfare began, victors brought home plunder seized from conquered people.

When the initial conflict was past, the exchange of styles and objects went back and forth between rulers and subjects, and then gradually spread beyond the original point of contact. For instance, in the fourth century B.C., Alexander the Great brought the style of classical Greece with him during conquests of Persia and the Middle East. There, traders from China carried classicism back home, and the Grecian influence soon became evident in Chinese pottery.

The entrance hall of a Florida house presents a polished, distinctive mix of streamlined twentieth-century furniture and stately Chinese chairs.

INTERIOR DESIGN
Geoffrey N. Bradfield

Photo: H. Durston Saylor

Centuries later, Napoleon relished the opportunity to incorporate in his own home the styles and wares of conquered lands. The French Empire style featured symbols of his subject countries, such as the Egyptian sphinx and imperial Roman eagle. On a somewhat happier note, marriage between royals from various European countries also led to mixing of styles, as did the rise of international commercial trade. The Victorians were particularly enthralled by the world that was opening up to them as merchant ships sailed the world, which translated into eclectic decor using objects from exotic places.

Although cross-cultural mixing is nothing new, what is new is that in times past the point of actual contact between the cultures often was several steps removed from the typical person who ended up with the object in his or her living room. Today, though, chances are a decorative item from Indonesia or Russia, Zimbabwe or Argentina, is part of a bigger story—the story of the owner's personal journey to a new culture, to a place that shed new perspective on living.

(left) An antique Chinese poly-chrome horse and numerous African objects give a home office an international perspective.

INTERIOR DESIGN

Justine Ringlien Interiors

Photo: Dennis Anderson

(below) A sense of Tuscany is evoked in this desert home, with a massive stone table and draped terra-cotta fabric resembling the texture of weathered Italian walls. Michelangelo's work is referenced in the painting.

INTERIOR DESIGN

McWhorter Associates

Photo: Arthur Coleman

This New York City residence
overlooking Central Park features a far-ranging collection of
artifacts that attests to the
owner's global travels.

INTERIOR DESIGN
*Designs by Billy W. Francis
and Ed Russell*

Photo: H. Durston Saylor

(left) Track lighting emphasizes the Chinese chest, whose simple form and golden wood tones complement the color of the leather upholstery and the lines of Mies van der Rohe's famous Barcelona furniture. Both the chest and the modern furniture are the best of their era.

INTERIOR DESIGN

Gandy/Peace

Photo: Chris A. Little

(below) Chinese artifacts and a lacquered chinoiserie low table add history and texture to a contemporary western setting.

INTERIOR DESIGN

Weixler, Peterson, & Luzi

Photo: Dan Forer

In this opulent dining room, the wallpaper hearkens to an exotic time and place. Scenic wallpapers became especially popular after trade with the Far East increased late in the seventeenth century.

INTERIOR DESIGN

Kenneth Hockin Interior Decoration

Photo: William Stites

(left) A virtual parade of figurines from Pakistan transforms a classic carved mantel.

INTERIOR DESIGN

Lloy Hack Associates

Photo: Eric Roth

(above) Decorative Oriental panels painted in exquisite colors enliven a New England dining room.

INTERIOR DESIGN

Ann Lenox

Photo: Steve Vierra

An antique German Biedermeier secretary and the Guatemalan *santo* in the foreground offer glimpses of two vastly different eighteenth-century cultures and a collector with equally divergent interests.

INTERIOR DESIGN

Carol Wolk Interiors

Photo: James W. Hedrich, Hedrich Blessing

(*left*) The bold colors of a Native American totem pole are carried through in the design of this highly original kitchen.

INTERIOR DESIGN

Elizabeth Munson

Photo: Steve Vierra

(*below*) Items from Asia, contemporary accents, and western antiques and reproductions come together in this pleasantly idiosyncratic space.

INTERIOR DESIGN

Lili Kray

Photo: Barry Kray

(below) The magnificent base of the dining-room table brings a distinct Oriental flavor to this residence. The chairs are in the style of Chippendale, who drew heavily on Chinese design.

INTERIOR DESIGN

Anne Tarasoff Interiors

Photo: Bill Rothschild

(right) In this inspired combination, a folding screen of eastern origin stands behind a sleigh bed whose design roots come from France.

INTERIOR DESIGN

Stacey Lapuk

Photo: John Sutton Photography

Neutral textiles and black accents complement an
antique Japanese screen.

INTERIOR DESIGN
Rodger Dobbel Interiors

Photo: Mark Darley

(below) Tribal arts and crafts from around the world give this den a distinctive ambiance and reveal the owner's passion for collecting primitive objects.

INTERIOR DESIGN

Kathy Guyton Interiors

Photo: David Schilling

(right) This room exemplifies the idea of a happy marriage between eastern and western styles, with the Chinese table set among overstuffed easy chairs and modern window accessories.

INTERIOR DESIGN

Antine Associates

Photo: Peter Paige

Pre-Columbian art mingles with an Oriental-style low
table and bamboo chairs.

INTERIOR DESIGN

Jennifer Garrigues

Photo: Barry Kinsella

(below) A bedroom that takes its inspiration from Japanese styles makes a serene retreat for a westerner drawn to the ethos of the East.

INTERIOR DESIGN

Marian Glasgow

Photo: Steve Vierra

(right) The warmth of ribbed upholstery and softly folded drapery serve as a backdrop for the cool stone of the carved torso and gleaming black sphinx.

INTERIOR DESIGN

Dale Carol Anderson

Photo: Tony Soluri

An Oriental chest and low table anchor either side of
this sunny room, a favorite spot for reading.

INTERIOR DESIGN

Henry Savage

Photo: Steve Vierra

Highly detailed furnishings and exotic
plants bring international flair to this home.

INTERIOR DESIGN

Rita St. Clair

Photo: Gordon Beall

(*left*) Allusions to ancient and exotic cultures add to the drama of this dining room.

INTERIOR DESIGN

Ron Wilson Designer

Photo: Mary Nichols

(*below*) This dining room's theme is crisp geometry, which is supported by the clean lines of the red Oriental chest.

INTERIOR DESIGN

Lovick Design

Photo: Art Grey

Alongside this living room's sofa, a sculpture
of a Chinese child is beloved by the owner
for its innocent, contented expression. A
golden sculpture of a head is reflected in
mirrored panels reminiscent of a Japanese
screen. From another angle (right), a collection of boxes can be seen on the coffee
table. The base of the table consists of capi-
tals from columns salvaged from a demol-
ished 1920s-vintage Florida house.

INTERIOR DESIGN

Al Evans Interiors

Photos: Dan Forer

Translucent screens modulate natural light
in this residence, where classic styles of the
Orient meet contemporary design.

INTERIOR DESIGN

Al Evans Interiors

Photo: Martin Fine

The lacquered screen and Chinese flower
pots incorporate more subtle versions of the
vivid color palette of this space.

INTERIOR DESIGN
Robert E. Tartarini Interiors

Photo: Dennis Krukowski

(left) The prints of Thailand inspired the sumptuous cotton upholstery and pillow fabric, adding a subtle Southeast Asian influence to an otherwise thoroughly western room.

Photo courtesy of Brunschwig & Fils

(below) Against the backdrop of a rich red wall, primitive masks crown this lofty study space and look down upon furnishings from centuries after their time.

INTERIOR DESIGN

John Robert Wiltgen Design

Photo: Jim Hedrich, Hedrich Blessing

(below) The sparseness of the Oriental aesthetic and contemporary art go hand in hand.

INTERIOR DESIGN

Celeste Cooper

Photo: Richard Mandelkorn

(right) The screen, chairs, and small statue of a wizened sage all point to the East, yet they are perfectly at home with the table's contemporary western aesthetic.

INTERIOR DESIGN

Rodger Dobbel Interiors

Photo: Mark Darley

The patterned fabrics are in keeping with the owner's
collection of African arts and crafts.

INTERIOR DESIGN

Celeste Cooper

Photo: Richard Mandelkorn

(below and opposite) This kitchen and its adjacent seating area succeed beautifully in mixing cross-cultural style with modern functionality.

INTERIOR DESIGN
Lloy Hack Associates

Photos: Edward C. Benner

(right) Baronial English-style architecture, a colorful beaded African table, Chinese pottery, and modern art combine in a room that attests to the owner's far-reaching travels.

INTERIOR DESIGN
McWhorter Associates

Photo: Joey Terrill

Some objects achieve the stature of a signature piece simply because they are rarely used as interior decoration. In this living space, an antique Chinese bamboo garment mounted on a cherry rod becomes the focal point.

INTERIOR DESIGN

Gandy/Peace

Photo: Chris A. Little

THE SIGNATURE ELEMENT

Some interiors, like some individuals, have a particular identifying characteristic that sets them apart. Rather than finding expression in the many, or a blend of numerous elements, they stand out because of the one, a single, fascinating quality.

When describing a person who has a signature style, few words are needed—"He always wears black." "She's artistic, and it comes out in her bold jewelry." "Hats are her trademark." When the signature approach works—whether in fashion or interior design—the image is striking and lingers in memory. When the look doesn't work, the one thing seems contrived, out-of-place, and, at worst, even silly.

In the world of interior design, what makes signature elements succeed? Here again, consider the basics of design and capitalize on them: line and form, texture and pattern, color and light, scale and proportion. Think about these basics not only regarding the object itself, but also in terms of context.

In your own home, one way to ease a signature piece toward the desired stature is by building similar surrounding themes, which then culminate with the focal item in a flourishing crescendo. When an exuberantly colored abstract painting is placed in a room dressed in pale tints of the same hues, the painting's magnificence is supported by the context. Another approach that almost always works is creating contrast between the signature element and the interior environment. Heads inevitably turn when an ornate, florid antique desk holds forth amid sleek, Spartan modernism. Next to polished steel and glass, the rough-hewn stone of an ages-old sculpture seems even more evocatively primitive.

Context is important, but a room's signature piece still needs to be remarkable in some way. The object intended to carry the day must have the wherewithal, the needed definition or intensity, to hold visual interest. If graceful lines are the piece's special quality, then they must be exquisitely beautiful. If the item shimmers with light, then its surface must indeed take on an ethereal glow. For an object to work as a signature element, it must confidently stand out, claiming center stage as eagerly as a diva on opening night.

Mirrors have a natural attraction (*below*), adding to the power of these ornate antique gilt frames mounted one within another. A distinctive pedestal table (*left*) serves to tie together the other pieces in this tailored living room.

INTERIOR DESIGN
Thomas Pheasant

Photos: Gordon Beall, courtesy of NSO Showhouse

(above) In a quiet contemporary bedroom characterized by crisp rectilinear geometry, the graceful undulation of an antique lounge elevates the piece to signature status.

INTERIOR DESIGN

Gandy/Peace

Photo: Chris A. Little

(right) This kitchen in an 1826 New England house has built-in warmth and a sense of history that is established by original wainscoting and pine floors. The owner's personal flair enters the equation with a contemporary print of a tropical fish, whose bold colors and graphic appeal anchor the room.

INTERIOR DESIGN

Carol Swift

Photo: Eric Roth

In this setting, the signature element comes as a pair—two
dramatic, asymmetrical chairs that carry the room's design.

INTERIOR DESIGN

Vince Lattuca, Visconti and Company

Photo: Bill Rothschild

Furnishings in this bedroom work together to support the
tropical mood established by the signature hand-painted
Japanese screen.

INTERIOR DESIGN

Designworks

Photo: Dan Forer

Soaring above the room, a mirror with classical themes
gains prominence through its placement.

INTERIOR DESIGN
Bierly-Drake Associates

Photo: Sam Gray

(below) Energy vibrates from the colorful geometry of the modern screen. Contemporary furniture complements the crisp look.

INTERIOR DESIGN
John Robert Wiltgen Design

Photo: Jeffery A. Atkins, Mercury Studios

(right) While some signature pieces gain even more emphasis when supported by similar but less dominant design elements, others stand out because they contrast with their surroundings. Here the background artwork is a world apart from the contemporary furniture.

Photo courtesy of Cassina USA

Bathed in natural light, the luminous girl in the signature painting seen through the arch is set against a background of earth tones, which are the foundation of the interior design palette.

INTERIOR DESIGN

Gary S. Gibson

Photo: Abel Mares

On top of its penetrating colors, forceful geometry, and
massive size, this abstract painting receives additional emphasis from lighting that is precisely placed and modulated.

INTERIOR DESIGN

Donna Dunn & Associates

Photo: Arthur Coleman

The elegant rooms shown on this page use two proven ways to emphasize a magnificent oversize object such as a painting or antique mirror—minimalist furnishings and a monochromatic background.

(left)
INTERIOR DESIGN
Veronique Louvet

Photo: Eric Roth

(below)
INTERIOR DESIGN
Fanny Haim and Benny Flint

Photo: Carlos Domenech

(below) The three dining companions in the delightfully quirky painting are bound to make a lasting impression at mealtime. The painting sets the tone for the space.

INTERIOR DESIGN
Bobbi Packer Designs

Photo: Bruce Van Inwegen

(right) A contemporary painting of bigger-than-life porcelain dishes anchors this dining room. The round Saarinen table echoes the shape of the dishes.

INTERIOR DESIGN
Lloy Hack Associates

Photo: Eric Roth

Against a brilliant red wall, the poster becomes the
room's focal point. Intense color draws the viewer's eye,
and the black frame and white border intensify the effect.

INTERIOR DESIGN

Lovick Design

Photo: Art Grey

A shimmering blue-and-gold antique robe is the main design attraction, reinforced by accents with the same highly saturated coloring. A collection of old leaded-glass windows adds interest while blending with the room's neutral background.

INTERIOR DESIGN
Ginny Stine Interiors

Photo: Neil Rashba

The Oriental screen not only ensures privacy and serves
as a bathroom rack for towels and robes, but it also has
the sheer panache to qualify as a signature piece.

INTERIOR DESIGN
Laura Bohn Design Associates

Photo: Phillip H. Ennis

(above and opposite) The screens with Chinese characters in both living room and dining room become memorable elements because of their size and unique design.

INTERIOR DESIGN
Antine Associates

Photos: Peter Paige

DIRECTORY OF DESIGNERS, MANUFACTURERS, AND PHOTOGRAPHERS

DESIGNERS AND MANUFACTURERS

Thomas C. Achille and Associates
521 North La Cienega Boulevard
Los Angeles, CA 90048

Francoise Theise
Adesso Furniture
200 Boylston Street
Boston, MA 02130

Dale Carol Anderson
2030 North Magnolia
Chicago, IL 60614

Antine Associates
1028 Arcadian Way
Fort Lee, NJ 07024

Auberge St. Antoine
10 rue St. Antoine
Quebec City, Quebec G1K 4C9
Canada

Nancy Tavel Balbus
700 Elkins Avenue, F2
Elkins Park, PA 19117

Bierly-Drake Associates, Inc.
17 Arlington Street
Boston, MA 02116

Laura Bohn Design Associates
30 West 26th
New York, NY 10010

Samuel Botero Associates
420 East 54th Street, Suite 34G
New York, NY 10022

Geoffrey Bradfield Inc.
105 East 63rd Street
New York, NY 10021

Brunschwig & Fils
979 Third Avenue
New York, NY 10022

Mario Buatta
120 East 80th Street
New York, NY 10021

Gayle Shaw Camden, ASID
Grosse Point, MI

Cann & Company
450 Harrison Avenue, Suite 417
Roxbury, MA 02118

Cassina USA
200 McKay Road
Huntington Station, NY 11746

CBT/Childs Bertman Tseckares
306 Dartmouth Street
Boston, MA 02116

Charles P. Rogers Brass
and Iron Beds
899 First Avenue
New York, NY 10022

Samantha Cole Interior Design
550 15th Street
San Francisco, CA 94103

Celeste Cooper, ASID
Repertoire
560 Harrison Avenue
Boston, MA 02118

James B. Coursey
Coursey Design Consultants
The Manse
Heath, MA 01346

Dakota Jackson, Inc.
979 Third Avenue, Suite 503
New York, NY 10022

Lilian Bogossian and Vivian Weil
Decorative Interiors
Route 7A
Manchester Village, VT 05254

Designworks Creative
Partnership, Ltd.
6501 Park of Commerce
Boulevard, Suite B205
Boca Raton, FL 33487

Barry Dixon
2019 Q Street Northwest
Washington, DC 20009

Rodger Dobbel Interiors
23 Vista Avenue
Piedmont, CA 94611

Constance Driscoll Design
Consultants
13 Dartmouth Street
Boston, MA 02116

Donna Dunn & Associates
73-230 Fiddleneck Lane
Palm Desert, CA 92260

Sarah C. Duquette
Duquette and Company
7 Lilac Lane
York Harbor, ME 03909

Arlis Ede Interiors
3520 Fairmount Street
Dallas, TX 75219

Al Evans Interiors Inc.
1001 South Bayshore Drive,
#2902
Miami, FL 33131

Jonathan Fishman, AIA
RCG, Inc.
2120 North Charles Street
Baltimore, MD 21218

Designs by Billy W. Francis
and Ed Russell
1100 North Alta Loma Road,
#1202
West Hollywood, CA 90069
and
800 Fifth Avenue, 11D
New York, NY 10021

Gandy/Peace Inc.
3195 Paces Ferry Place
Atlanta, GA 30305

Jennifer Garrigues
308 Peruvian Avenue
Palm Beach, FL 33480

Gary S. Gibson
511 North La Cienega, Suite 202
Los Angeles, CA 90048

Marian Glasgow Interiors
9 Laurel Street
Newton Centre, MA 01776

Ida Goldstein
16 Munnings Drive
Sudbury, MA 01776

Susan Zises Green
11 East 44th Street
New York, NY 10017

Marcia Connors and Roxy Gray
Growing Spaces
4 Fall Lane
Canton, MA 02021

Claude Guidi
411 East 57th Street
New York, NY 10022

Kathy Guyton Interiors
55 Bennett Street, Suite 20
Atlanta, GA 30309

Lloy Hack Associates Inc.
425 Boylston Street
Boston, MA 02116

Haim, Flint & Associates, Inc.
21338 West Dixie Highway
North Miami Beach, FL 33180

Kenneth Hockin Interior
Decoration
Old Chelsea Station
P. O. Box 1117
New York, NY 10011

Henry Johnstone & Co.
95 San Miguel Road
Pasadena, CA 91105

C & J Katz Studio
135 Myrtle Street
Boston, MA 02114

Lili Kray, ASID/FIIDA
1855 Merchandise Mart
Chicago, IL 60654

Susan Kroeger Ltd.
253 Franklin Street
Glencoe, IL 60022

Stacey Lapuk Interior Design, Inc.
3 Friars Lane
Mill Valley, CA 94941

Ann Lenox, ASID
Partners In Design
860 Walnut Street
Newton Centre, MA 02159

Veronique Louvet
66 Haskell Street
Beverly Farms, MA 01915

Lovick Design
11339 Burnham Street
Los Angeles, CA 90049

Jack E. Lowrance
Lowrance Interiors, Inc.
707 North Alfred Street
Los Angeles, CA 90069

Judith Lynne Interior Design
P. O. Box 4998
Palm Springs, CA 92263

Paul Magnuson
10 Central Street
Beverly, MA 01915

Judy McMurray
Interiors Editions
South Road R.R.3, Box 165
Hopkinton, NH 03229

William F. McWhorter
McWhorter Associates
1041 1/2 South Genesee Avenue
Los Angeles, CA 90019

Rodgers Menzies Interior Design
766 South White Station Road,
Suite 5
Memphis, TN 38117

Anna Meyers Interiors
162 West Huron
Chicago, IL 60610

Sandra Nunnerley Inc.
112 East 71st Street
New York, NY 10021

Olson Lewis & Dioli Architects
17 Elm Street
Manchester-by-the-Sea, MA 01944

Bobbi Packer Designs
126 Edgecliff Drive
Highland Park, IL 60033

Thomas Pheasant, Inc.
1029 33rd Street Northwest
Washington, DC 20007

Josef Pricci Ltd.
737 Park Avenue
New York, NY 10021

Annelle Primos & Associates
4500 I–55 North, Suite 126
Jackson, MS 39211

Andrew Reczkowski
102 Watts Street
Chelsea, MA 02150

Justine Ringlien Interiors
96 Ridgeview Drive
Atherton, CA 94027

Deborah M. Roub
Shade of the Elm
P. O. Box 519
Limerick, ME 04048

Justine Sancho
4827 Fairmont Avenue
Bethesda, MD 20814

Henry Savage Jr., ASID
Creative Images Limited
20 Park Plaza, Suite 453
Boston, MA 02116

Freya Serabian Design Associates
36 Church Street
Winchester, MA 01890

Sally Sirkin Interior Design
8727 Melrose Avenue
Los Angeles, CA 90069

Howard Snoweiss Design Group
4200 Aurora Street, Suite D
Coral Gables, FL 33146

Jose Solis Betancourt
Solis Betancourt
1054 Potomac Street Northwest
Washington, DC 20007

Dawn Southworth and Dana Salvo
63 Bennett Street
Gloucester, MA 01930

Charles Spada
65 East India Row
Boston, MA 02110

Elizabeth Speert, Inc.
53 Barnard Avenue
Watertown, MA 02172

Rita St. Clair Associates
1009 North Charles Street
Baltimore, MD 21201

Stedila Design
135 East 55th Street
New York, NY 10022

Ginny Stine Interiors, Inc.
1936 San Marco Boulevard
Jacksonville, FL 32207

Stingray Hornsby Interior Design
5 The Green
Watertown, CT 06795

Karen Sugarman Interiors
185 North Main Street
Andover, MA 01810

Anne Tarasoff Interiors
25 Andover Road
Port Washington, NY 11050

Robert E. Tartarini Interiors
P. O. Box 293
Old Westbury, NY 11568

Stan Topol & Associates Inc.
1100 Spring Street, Suite 400
Atlanta, GA 30309

Jean Valente Inc.
175 East 79th Street
New York, NY 10021

Vince Lattuca
Visconti and Company
245 East 57th Street
New York, NY 10021

Alfred J. Walker Fine Art
158 Newbury Street
Boston, MA 02116

Weixler, Peterson & Luzi
2031 Locust Street, Suite GFWR
Philadelphia, PA 19103

Camille Belmonte and
Mary Beth Galvin
Wellesley Design Center
868 Worcester Road
Wellesley, MA 02181

Ron Wilson, Designer
1235 Tower Road
Beverly Hills, CA 90210

John Robert Wiltgen Design
70 West Hubbard, #205
Chicago, IL 60610

Vicente Wolf Associates, Inc.
333 West 39th Street
New York, NY 10018

Carol Wolk Interiors Ltd.
340 Tudor Court
Glencoe, IL 60022

Mark Zeff Consulting Group Inc.
260 West 72nd Street
New York, NY 10023

PHOTOGRAPHERS

Jean Allsopp
1504 Grove Place
Birmingham, AL 35209

Dennis Anderson
48 Lucky Drive
Greenbrae, CA 94904

Jaime Ardiles-Arce
140 East 56th Street
New York, NY 10022

Jeffery A. Atkins
Mercury Studios, Inc.
2548 West Cortez Street
Chicago, IL 60622

Gordon Beall
4507 Sangamore Road, #101
Bethesda, MD 20816

Edward C. Benner
227 Coolidge Avenue
Watertown, MA 02172

Steven Brooke
7910 Southwest 54 Court
Miami, FL 33143

Arthur Coleman
303 North Indian Canyon Drive
Palm Springs, CA 92262

Mark Darley
23 Midway Avenue
Mill Valley, CA 94941

Carlos Domenech
6060 Southwest 26th Street
Miami, FL 33155

Phillip H. Ennis
98 Smith Street
Freeport, NY 11520

Dan Forer
6815 Southwest 81st Terrace
Miami, FL 33143

Michael Garland
26 28th Avenue
Venice, CA 90291

Sam Gray
23 Westwood Road
Wellesley, MA 02181

Hedrich Blessing
11 West Illinois Street
Chicago, IL 60610

Alec Hemer
81 Bedford Street, Apartment 5E
New York, NY 10014

Christopher Irion
183 Shipley Street
San Francisco, CA 94107

Warren Jagger Photography
150 Chestnut Street
Providence, RI 02903

Tom Joynt
741 Harris Street, Suite E
Jackson, MS 39202

Ethan Kaminsky
870 Research Drive
Palm Springs, CA 92262

Rob Karosis Photography
855 Islington Street, Suite 7
Portsmouth, NH 03801-4270

Balthazar Korab
5051 Beach Road
Troy, MI 48098

Barry Kray
4300 Ponchartrain
New Buffalo, MI 49117

Dennis Krukowski
329 East 92nd Street,
Apartment 1D
New York, NY 10128

Andrew D. Lautman
Lautman Photography
4906 41st Street Northwest
Washington, DC 20016

Chris A. Little
P. O. Box 467221
Atlanta, GA 30346

David Livingston
1036 Erica Road
Mill Valley, CA 94941

Richard Mandelkorn Photography
65 Beaver Pond Road
Lincoln, MA 01773

Abel Mares
2212-B Glendale Boulevard
Los Angeles, CA 90039

Deborah Mazzoleni
21012 West Liberty Road
White Hall, MD 21161

Ira Montgomery
2406 Converse
Dallas, TX 75207

Mary Nichols
323 North Arden Boulevard
Los Angeles, CA 90004

Peter Paige
269 Parkside Road
Harrington Park, ND 07640

Neil Rashba
2719 Stardust Court
Jacksonville, FL 32207

Kevin C. Rose
Rose Studio, Inc.
146 Walker Street
Atlanta, GA 30313

Steve Rosenthal Photography
59 Maple Street
Auburndale, MA 02166

Eric Roth Studio
337 Summer Street
Boston, MA 02210

Bill Rothschild
19 Judith Lane
Wesley Hills, NY 10952

Mario Ruiz
7 Elybrook To Hands Creek Road
East Hampton, NY 11937

H. Durston Saylor
175 5th Avenue
New York, NY 10010

David Schilling
1816-D Briarwood Ind. Court
Atlanta, GA 30329

Walter Smalling Photography
1541 8th Street Northwest
Washington, DC 20001

Tony Soluri
1147 West Ohio, Suite 403
Chicago, IL 60622

William Stites
1075 75th Street
Marathon, FL 33050

John Sutton Photography
8 Main Street
Point San Quentin, CA 94964

Joey Terrill
18653 Ventura Boulevard,
Suite 135
Tarzana, CA 91356

Bruce Van Inwegen
5427 North Bernard Street
Chicago, IL 60625

Alexander Vertikoff
P. O. Box 2079
Tejeras, NM 87059

Steve Vierra Photography
P. O. Box 1827
Sandwich, MA 02563

Peter Vitali
P. O. Box 2086
Santa Fe, NM 87504

Charles White
154 North Mansfield Avenue
Los Angeles, CA 90036

ABOUT THE AUTHOR

Carol Meredith writes about interior design and architecture for magazines, newspapers, and professional design firms. During her fifteen years in the field, she has served as managing editor for *Texas Homes* and home and garden editor for *New England Living* magazine. Ms. Meredith's articles about interior design also have been published in *Design Times, Boston* magazine, and the *Boston Globe.* She currently lives in New Hampshire, where she shares a home with her husband, David Reynolds, and stepdaughters Anne and Aleisha.